Language of Love

Debbie Brewster

Copyright © 2023 by Debbie Brewster

All rights reserved. No part of this publication may be reproduced, stored in a retrieval system, or transmitted in any form or by any means--electronic, mechanical, photocopying, recording, or otherwise--without the prior written permission of the publisher or copyright owner.

This is a work of fiction. Any resemblance to any place or person is unintended and purely coincidental.

After a long nine months of anticipating our family's new arrival, the day had finally come. It was a cool spring evening in April, when we found ourselves welcoming my new little brother. We could hardly contain the excitement that he was finally here. He was like a new toy that everyone wanted to hold. We all took turns passing him around, even me.

There was a lot going on in that small hospital room. All the smiles and laughter, flashes from cameras, and everyone making comments as to who he looked most like. It was a moment we would all remember. How exciting! I finally had a new 7 pound 9 ounce baby brother, who my parents had decided to name, Stephen.

We had to wait a couple days before we could finally bring him home.

He was the smallest member in our family, but the loudest of all by far!

He seemed to cry when he was hungry, when his diaper needed changed,

when he was sleepy, and all the time in between.

It seemed like a chain reaction. He would cry, and someone would pick him up and start babbling and cooing, as if to speak in some unknown language. Whatever it was he seemed to understand it. He seemed much calmer as if, all of those silly noises gave him comfort. He would quit crying and open his eyes as if he was trying to hear every sound that was being made. I didn't understand why everyone in the family would entertain him in such a manner, when he clearly couldn't make sense out of any of that. Those silly noises that seemed to turn adults into babbling idiots. How would Stephen ever learn to speak properly?

One day we went to my grandpas for a visit. Grandpa and I always played cards, or went for walks, or sung songs together. We were always doing something fun. I knew Grandpa was always just as excited for our visit as we were. Stephen was a few months old at this time. He still cried a lot but not as often as before (or possibly, I had just gotten more used to hearing it).

When mom laid Stephen into Grandpa's arms, Grandpas face lit up. He was bubbling over with funny noises and silly faces. What had happened to Grandpa? Who was this man? It was like he had lost all his senses and was acting like a silly child. Although his behavior had me puzzled, he had Stephen laughing and cooing so loudly. It was so weird, but yet funny to watch them imitate each other. Grandpa would make a funny noise, and Stephen would try to make a noise as if they had invented a new language all of their very own. I watched and listened patiently, because I knew it would soon be my turn to play with Grandpa. It didn't take long till Stephen had fallen asleep. He just laid peacefully in Grandpa's gentle but strong, loving arms. Those same arms that hugged, carried, and comforted me, were now comforting my little brother.

After Grandpa laid Stephen down, it was my time with Grandpa. I knew he always took the time to listen and talk with me. I thought it was the perfect time to ask a question that was running through my mind.

"Grandpa," I said, "what makes people act so different around babies? It's like they seem to lose all their senses and act silly, and no longer act like adults."

Grandpa began to chuckle as he started to explain to me that, although Stephen couldn't understand words that were spoken to him yet, the sounds still calmed him and made him happy. He wasn't afraid. It was as if he found comfort in knowing someone was there and he wasn't alone. He may not recognize the words we spoke or understand their meanings, but some things didn't have to be spoken to be understood. It was through the gentle, caring ways we treated him that made him feel comforted. At that stage in his life, he would understand more from our actions than he would from our words. It was like it was his very own special language that he could understand, no matter how strange it seemed to me.

I learned a lot of things about family and life from Grandpa as I was growing up. My parents made sure that we understood the value of family. We may not have had a lot of material things, but we had each other. Family was a gift that not everyone had, so we couldn't take it for granted. We spent lots of time together. We went on vacations, had picnics by the fishing hole, played games. We were always doing something fun and exciting together. We were making memories that we could share for years to come. I would always have my family. We would always be together. It was such a comforting thought that brought a smile to my face every time.

Life was good growing up with Grandpa. He lived on a farm. Stephen and I would go with him to gather eggs and feed the chickens. We spent countless hours sitting at Grandpa's feet listening to stories about his childhood. Sometimes, I think he made them up or added funny details to make us laugh, but either way, we always enjoyed hearing whatever it was he had to say. We would watch the expressions on his face change and the tone in his voice would go up and down with excitement. He was the best storyteller. We hung on every word. We loved Grandpa, and he loved us. We enjoyed being with him no matter what we were doing. He made it fun.

One day, we were out on a walk, taking a path that we had taken many times before, but this time was a little different. Grandpa for some reason pretended that he didn't know his way home. He was such a kidder. We knew he was testing us to see if we could find our way back to the house. We held Grandpa's hands, Stephen on one side and I on the other, as we led him back home. When we walked into the kitchen, Mom asked where we had been. Stephen and I proceeded to tell her about our walk and how Grandpa had pretended that he didn't know the way back. We were so proud of ourselves that we had passed Grandpa's test.

Later that week we went to visit Grandpa again. As always, he met us with a big smile on his face. He was always waiting with a big bear hug as he called us by name and welcomed us in. This time, though, he had gotten our names mixed up. He was always being funny, but today it seemed as though he was being more silly than usual and pretending to be more forgetful.

As we went into the kitchen, we noticed that Grandpa's favorite tromping boots were covered with mud and sitting on the table. When we asked him why he had put them there, he said that he hadn't, and he wasn't even sure whose boots they were. My mom quickly removed the boots and took them outside to clean them up. The rest of the day, Stephen and I had fun visiting with Grandpa. Our parents seemed a little distracted though, like they were worried about something. How could they possibly be upset when we were having such a great time with Grandpa?

A couple months went by, and Grandpa seemed to be acting even more differently. He seemed to be changing. He was getting things more confused, and it seemed as if he was always sad. That was so unlike Grandpa. My parents decided that he needed to go to the doctor to see why he was acting so strangely. Stephen and I were beginning to get worried at this time because we had never known Grandpa to be sick, let alone cry or be unhappy. What could be wrong with Grandpa?

When Mom and Grandpa returned from the doctor's office, we all ran out to the car to meet them. Dad went behind the car with Mom. They were whispering about something for a moment, so Stephen and I walked hand-in-hand with Grandpa back to the house. We thought Grandpa seemed fine. He wasn't coughing or complaining of a belly ache so he must be okay now. The doctor must have made him feel all better.

That evening after we returned home, our parents sat us down and explained to us that Grandpa was beginning to get things confused. His confusion wasn't just him playing around with us anymore. He was having problems with simple, everyday tasks. The things he used to remember were getting more and more difficult to recall, and simple things weren't making sense to him. They told us that, if he said things that seemed a bit mixed up, not to try to correct him, but to let him continue his stories even if they made no sense. In Grandpas mind it would all make sense. We didn't really understand all the things that Mom was trying to tell us, but we would be patient with Grandpa just the same.

A few months later, as we were on our way to see Grandpa, mom said she had a special surprise. We would be bringing grandpa home with us for a few days. Since Grandpa didn't come to have a sleepover very often, this was going to be a real treat! We were excited; however, I'm not sure Grandpa shared the same enthusiasm. He and my parents seemed to be disagreeing about something in the back room. Stephen and I had no idea what was going on, but we kept hearing Grandpa say he was too busy to come for a visit. I guess they worked it all out though, because when we left, Grandpa came too. That visit lasted much longer than ever before, but we didn't mind. It was nice having him with us.

As months passed, we noticed Grandpa getting quieter. He started saying more things that made no sense and started having a hard time speaking. He was also having a difficult time getting dressed and never wanted to take a bath. It was so unlike the Grandpa that we had known all our life. He wasn't as fun to be around anymore.

Things he did were funny at times, but he didn't laugh. He didn't seem to understand when we would do something funny or tell him a story. It was like he was in his own world. He would call me Susan (which was my mother's name) and talk about how I was older than he was and recall things we used to do way before I was born. Grandpa certainly had things mixed up. It was hard seeing him like this. What had happened to Grandpa?

Our parents finally explained to us that Grandpa had a kind of crippling mind disease. It was called Dementia, and over time, it would continue to get worse. Grandpa would be more and more confused.

About a year later, the reality of what our parents had tried to prepare us for was staring us in the face. Grandpa had gone from dementia to something called Alzheimer's. He had forgotten how to do simple things like comb his hair or brush his teeth. He even needed help going to the bathroom, getting a bath, and getting dressed.

By the time I was a teenager, I had distanced myself from Grandpa. He had gotten boring and required a lot of assistance. He wasn't fun anymore, and I had lots of other things to do. I didn't have time to listen to him talk nonsense or watch him stare out the window.

Our parents' lives had become so busy with taking care of Grandpa. They wanted him to live with us so they could take care of him, but as time went by, he needed more assistance than even my parents could give. Sadly, we had to move Grandpa into a nursing home facility a few miles down the road. It was a hard adjustment for our family, even for Stephen and me. We may not have spent much time with him now, but we found comfort in knowing he was there. After all, he was part of our family.

Mom took the move the hardest of all. She cried a lot and felt like she had let Grandpa down. She didn't want him to think that she didn't love him anymore.

She tried to go see him every day and take him special treats. Sometimes, Mom would pick him wildflowers, as those were his favorite. She would feed him and wash his face and spent countless hours just sitting beside him holding his hand. She even opened his curtains so that the sun would shine in and make his room bright. She tried her best to make things comfortable for Grandpa and spend as much time with him as she could. Mom even tried to get Stephen and I to go see him, but we were too busy. We just didn't have the time to go sit beside him and stare at four walls. That just wasn't fun.

One day Stephen and I asked mom why she went to see Grandpa every day even though he didn't know who she was or where he was even at. Mom just smiled at first, and as a tear rolled down her cheek, she told us to sit down beside her. Dad sat with us and held Mom's hand as she choked back the tears. She asked me if I remembered when Stephen was a baby and couldn't talk yet.

I said "Yes, I remember, he didn't understand anything at first."

Grandpa said we had to talk to him in a language that he understood even if it seemed a little strange to us."

Mom just smiled, and repeated my words, "a language he understood."

"Not all things have to be spoken, she said, It's how we treated him that let him know he was cared for and loved even before he could speak or really understand the words. We didn't ignore him or give up on him, we took the time to care for him and spent time with him. How do you think that made him feel?"

I thought for a moment and said, "He probably felt warm inside, and happy. Like he was right where he was supposed to be, he belonged with us."

Mom smiled again.

She continued to explain that when she was a baby, Grandpa treated her special, just like he had both of us. Grandpa made sure that we had wonderful memories and knew without a doubt that we would always have the love of family even if we had nothing else."

"Yes, it's true that Grandpa may have his memories mixed up now," she said. "He may not know who we are, but we do know who he is."

"He is the same man who spoke a crazy language with us as babies, and made funny faces because he wanted to see us smile. Even when we didn't know what we ourselves were doing, he did."

"He's the same man who bounced us on his knee and cradled us in his arms when we were tired, sleepy, or not feeling well. He fed us when we couldn't feed our self and washed our faces when we were messy. It was important to him that we knew he loved us. He showed us his love in many different ways, even without words. He didn't have to say a thing, we just knew."

She continued as we all were wiping tears from our eyes, "Now Grandpa is still a part of our family. He would still want to show us that he loves us, but he doesn't know how to anymore. It's our turn to show him the kind of love that he has always shown us, even if he doesn't respond as we would like. He deserves the same love and respect he gave us when he spoke our special language years ago."

What mom had said, made us think. Especially me, as I was the oldest. I really needed to go see Grandpa and take every opportunity I had left to make sure he felt loved. Even if one day or one moment was all he would remember, I wanted it to be a good memory. I wanted him to know he was still very loved.

I tried to visit him as often as I could. Some days, he smiled and muttered a few words, and other days, he was silent and seemed to be distant, as if he was in his own little world. He may have no longer understood the meaning of my words, but I know he felt the love, just the same. It was once again a special language that he understood. His face would light up when he saw me smile, heard my voice, or when I gave him a hug. It wasn't important that he no longer recognized my face or knew my name, besides, he didn't even remember his own name anymore. The important thing was that I still knew who he was, and he wasn't alone. He felt safe and loved.

Days with Grandpa were not the same as they were when we were younger, but every visit provided a new opportunity to share a part of our life with him. To share a new story, a new joke, or take him a card or a handpicked wildflower. To open his window and share the sunshine… or share an ice cream cone… or maybe even take a stroll down the hall together. To Grandpa, we might just have been the face of a stranger… but I'm sure deep down inside, his heart recognized us as friendly messengers speaking that old familiar language… the Language of Love.

About the Author

Debbie Brewster wrote Language of Love in the hopes of encouraging families and friends to pull together when one of their own is fighting a battle with the terrible disease, Alzheimer's.

Memory loss for someone doesn't mean we stop making memories. Even though a loved one may forget who they are—or who we are—we should never forget the special role they have had in our lives. They are still the one who gifted us with their time, adding to our precious memories.

While there are medications and management strategies to help deal with this awful condition, the best defense in this battle is a loving support group. Family and friends who don't leave a loved one to fight alone.

Debbie is a Christian, saved by Grace; a wife to her loving husband of thirty-six years, Freddie; a mother to her amazing son, Greg; a bonus mom to Greg's beautiful wife, Ashley; and a Grand-Mommy to her adorable, sweet, loving, precious, grandson, Odin Titus Brewster.

Acknowledgements

To my family for their love and encouragement to publish Language of Love. I am very blessed!

*

To all of those special people in my life who have, and are, fighting a good fight in the battle of Alzheimer's. A special "hug" to Karen Jones, a dear friend who I march alongside while she fights the battle at this very time.

*

To Robert M. Kerns, the Writer / Publisher of Knightsfall Press, who helped to push me out of my comfort zone to not only publish my story but also do my own illustrations. Thank you, Rob, for all of your work in making Language of Love come into print.

*

To God who loves us and watches over us all. He never leaves us to fight any battle alone.

www.ingramcontent.com/pod-product-compliance
Lightning Source LLC
Chambersburg PA
CBHW040301100526
44585CB00005BA/127